DOSHIE MAE

By

C. S. MORROW

Bloomington, IN  Milton Keynes, UK

authorHOUSE®

AuthorHouse™
1663 Liberty Drive, Suite 200
Bloomington, IN 47403
www.authorhouse.com
Phone: 1-800-839-8640

AuthorHouse™ UK Ltd.
500 Avebury Boulevard
Central Milton Keynes, MK9 2BE
www.authorhouse.co.uk
Phone: 08001974150

First published by AuthorHouse 1/4/2007

ISBN: 978-1-4259-7392-6 (sc)

Library of Congress Control Number: 2006909449

Printed in the United States of America
Bloomington, Indiana

This book is printed on acid-free paper.

Dedication

This book is dedicated to my mother, Doshie Lillie Mae Morrow. She's always been my most ardent supporter and kindest critic. The perseverance she's shown through the many challenges and hardships she's faced has proven to be an example of courage and strength to all of her children, grandchildren and great-grandchildren. Through it all, she has maintained an incredibly gentle and loving spirit. I Love You, Mama.

Letter to Myself

Tonight, he upset me again. He was supposed to be at home with his daughter, but instead he calls and tells me he's at a club/bar with his best friend.....that's what he says. It may or may not be true. I really don't care. I'm tired of him and the drama.

He cheated on me. Lied to me so many times I can't even count. Lying comes naturally to him so I never knew when he was telling the truth. We were physically violent towards eachother, which is not like me at all. No one has ever treated me that way and I've never raised my hand to anyone, either. And to be perfectly honest, he never really did anything for me. I had all the money, all the resources, all the brains but he had all the power. That makes no sense. Knowing all of that, I've been with this fool for 2 years. Why?

I honestly don't know. I know at one point I wanted to believe that I could change him, make him a better person. I thought I could fix all that had happened to him in the past and make him love me the way I loved him. I thought if I could show him how to love, show him how to be responsible, show him how to be a man, he'd take these lessons and apply them in our relationship. I thought there would eventually be some benefit to me being with him. I could not have been more wrong.

In recent months, I've started to feel my power, my strength come back. He'd broken me down to the point I never thought I could be happy again. It's a sad thing to see someone live in constant misery...that was me. All I could do was cry and worry, worry and cry. But over the past few months, I've come to realize that I'm much happier when I'm not with him, when I'm not thinking about him. I come home, relax in my most comfortable chair, read a book, watch the Golden Girls or Cold Case, and I am so very content. And he barely enters my mind during these moments.

And when he does hurtful things, yes, I still get hurt. But I don't cry anymore. He hasn't changed over the years so as far as I'm concerned, I have no reason to cry. I know him. I know what he's like. And I've accepted his behavior up to this point so when he does these things, why cry? They're no surprise anymore. Why cry? It's not like he's never done these things to me before. Why cry? When I have chosen to stay.

I had chosen to believe that he loved me, would take care of me. He needed me so I was going to stay by his side and take care of him. Why would I take care of someone who hasn't taken care of me and never will? Why would I want to stay by his side when I know that when push comes to shove, he will not be there for me?

Tonight I'm giving up. When he called and said those hurtful things to me, I almost cried. But then I stopped myself. I forbade myself to cry. I got angry at myself for feeling like crying. Haven't I given him enough of my tears? Why cry over something I lost, when I never really had it? I tried to call him back so I could make him talk to me, make him hear what I had to say. I stopped myself. What is there to say? I won't say anything I haven't said before and neither will he. So why am I going to disturb my peaceful evening and fill it with drama. I even texted a few bitter messages to his cell phone....it's not like it's going to change him or anything that he has or will do. So I stopped. I called a few friends, watched one of my favorite tv shows and wrote this letter.

I will not cry myself to sleep, I will not sit in the house and cry, depressed over him. Tomorrow will be a beautiful day and I'm going to enjoy it....even if it's pouring down raining. I'm going to enjoy tomorrow and every day after that. I'm moving on to a new, more healthy relationship...an everlasting love affair...with myself.

He was never worth my time, my love, my spirit, my energy. I knew soon after I met him that he wasn't for me but I made the mistake of trying to force the situation and look where it got me.

But I'm not going to be mad at him or myself. That, too, would require too much energy.

I have an ailing mother that I need to treasure while I still have the opportunity. I have a loving family, even though some of them are a little crazy. I have the most beautiful friends anyone could ever hope for. I have a job that I love and I'm starting school in a few weeks, pursuing my life-long dream of becoming a forensic scientist. What do I have to cry or be sad about? Not much. I deserve to be happy and I will be.

I will not change my mind. I will not second guess myself. I will not argue with him about my decision or spend time trying to justify it. I will not let him goad me into continuing the relationship. And if I ever feel like I'm going to change my mind and go back to him, I will read this letter over and over, until I come back to my senses.

My only regret is that I didn't recognize my power/strength and use it sooner. My only fear is that by him violating my trust, I might have been exposed to something unfavorable. But again, I have too many other things to be thankful for so I'm not going to worry about these things or dwell on them. I will leave all of that (and him) to the Lord.

Contents

Empties

I've got the Empties
Do you know what that means?

Empty mind
Empty stares
Full of holes
but no one cares

About a girl
Or her Empty life
Empty Days
Empty Nights

Empty Heart
Empty Soul
Empty Arms
No 1 to hold

Have you ever been
Or are you
Empty?

Hats Off

Bravo, Baby!
Bravo!
Come, now-
Now is not the time to be modest, My Dear
It doesn't suit you AT ALL
Accept your Kudos—-You Must!
I'll have it no other way
The verbal bashing has finally paid off
I've gone MAD
Unmistakably
Irreversibly
MAD
I have to commend you
You play an excellent game of emotional ping-pong
The Best, really
But I'm not angry
Please—erase that thought from your pretty little head
of yours
I'm anything But
You see, Madness gives one a whole new take on things
For instance, I'm no longer shackled by the rights
AND the wrongs
I do what I please
Consequences?
I don't know what those are
So it's perfectly alright for me to do
What I'm about to do
To You

On My Way

If I ever said I love you
I meant it
I love you no less today
But love won't right past wrongs
Nor will it prevent those I know will come
The disappointments are too frequent
Good Times are scarce
I wish you no hurt or harm
Only Love
Still, I have to get gone
You've presented no alternative
'Sorry' only goes so far

The Source

It's a feeling like no other
can't get it from sis or mother
never from daddy or brother
the only Source is you

the feeling comes from deep within
originates in each cell, flows out my skin
never enough, please give it again
keep doin' what you do

Touch me, Lover, Touch me sweet
touch the sweetest part of me
touch me slow, touch me deep
prove your love is true

INTUITION

Being my first friend
Lifelong confidant
she knows me like no other
knows me like only a Mother can
so when she asks what's troubling her babe
Why does my mood darken?
I can not lie
so I reply——"I just don't feel well"
that's only a half truth
my physical state reflects what I'm feeling within
but how can I break my Mother's heart?
By telling
How lonely and sad
Hurt and mad
How helpless and depressed
Utterly unhappy and stressed
I really am
I seek her comfort and understanding
but at the same time I'm afraid of it
Afraid that upon revealing my sorrow
and receiving her emotional gifts
I'll create unrest in her heart
It's only natural for a Mother to feel that way
My confession would ricochet
and be yet another source of pain for me
So I stick to my story
Feigning physical ills
Deep down, she knows and she'll worry
But for what, she does not know
I'll never justify her concerns

No Play

Why does it have to be
lies, tricks, deceit
I'm so tired of all the fucking games

Don't bother to approach me
try to get to know me
or ask for my number and my name

If all you're good for is Nothing
If you ain't saying something
that I can take to the bank

Keep that bullshit to yourself
it's hazardous to my health
just keep walking and I'll be on my way

Dreams of David

Last night I dreamt of David
we kissed
He told me He loved me
and held me
it felt wonderful to be so close to him again
yet I couldn't stop crying
because I knew he'd eventually let go
when I awoke, there were no tears
my heart was still full
my heart was still broken
hours after I woke, the tears came
and all I want to do is sleep
because that's the only way
I could ever hope to see him again

Victim

Who hurt you today?

was it your boss who wrote you up
for being 10 minutes late
was it the bill collector who called
because you had not bothered to pay

was it the repo man who took your car
because you didn't pay the note
was it the cop who wrote you a ticket
for being in the No Parking zone

was it your sister who told you
she had no money for your hand
or was it me who told you
to grow up and be a Man

........................or anything

It's not like we're an item or anything
but you've become part of me
you're too sweet not to be
that's why it hurts me to know
that I've hurt you
don't ask why
there's not been an excuse created
that's good enough to explain
But I am sorry
sorry to have lost a friend
sorry to have wounded you, sweet boy
not that I love you or anything
but I miss you

Kiss Me

Your lips are like the month of May

A little warm
A little wet

So kiss me

Changes

what do you do when things just don't look the same?
faces marked with disappointment and regret
sore hearts
dark spirits
how does it all go on?
how do we continue?
can we continue?
betrayal changes everything

Where Are You?

When it's party time
And you're in the mood for fun
Where are you?
When you have money to squander
And you're in the mood to impress
..can't find you
When you're low
When you're tired, hungry, scared
Or otherwise in need
I know exactly where you'll be
You'll come running to me
So I can make it all better
So I can save you
Again
No More
Mommy's all tapped out
I don't want a piece of you
I don't want the broken you
I want all of you
Or I don't want you at all

Zero

10 days since the revelation
9:00 pm, July 15th, we officially ended
8 months 'til I'm due
7 poems I've written so far
6 years since I last felt this way
5 days I lamented
4 days since I've seen you
3 days since we've spoken
Twice you betrayed me
Once again, I'm alone

NumLock

D5d y64 2n6w
D5d 5 te33 y64
5t's n6t s6 easy t6 say
B4t 5 th5n2 5 05ght
Be fa335ng
F6r y64
5 a0 s6 4tter3y
S6 c60*3ete3y
Ena06red
S6 tr43y
4nd64bted3y
F433
6f want
F6r y64
3et
0e 36ve y64

To Be a Woman

Life's experiences
have made me cautious but I still take chances
I'm wise, not omniscient
my skin is tough, not impenetrable
my heart has been hardened, not yet turned to stone
I'm independent
but there are times I need someone special,
need to feel special
I Want to be touched
I Long to be wooed
This is how it is to be a Woman

They Don't Know

They don't know what I know
They'll never know how special I feel
No matter how many times I tell them
I could sadly say to them:
'I have more Love in one place than some of you will ever know'
It's only sad because I wish they could have it, too
I could tell them of years of sacrifice and struggle
That didn't have to be endured, but were
But even if I said all that, they still wouldn't know
They have seen more beautiful places than I have
Some may have even seen more beautiful things than I have
But none of this matters
Because I have seen a more beautiful person than they have
Her skin no longer has that youthful glow
That's ok, though, because I shine for her
Her legs may be tired
That's still ok
Because I'm willing to walk that extra mile
Crystals of ice may creep through her hair
Even that's ok because everyone knows that the sun always sparkles
brightest when beaming through the face of a crystal
Do you know why they still don't know
After all of this?
Because, Mother, they don't know you

To the Man I Love

Nature knows you well
Your eyes sparkle like stars,
Glistening in the night.
As I gaze into them,
I wish that you were mine.
With lips as full as the moon
I long to feel them pressed against mine.
You are a strong man.
Black in every way.
Your strength lifts me up --
as if I were but a frail leaf
caught in a windstorm.
You are passionate, but gentle.
Your rhythms roll within me,
just as the tears roll down my face when we're apart.
We need eachother
Just as air is necessary for life
We are necessary for each other
I Love You.

Lilly

Lilly looks so sad
She's just a baby
but she has the weary look of an elder
Lilly walks up and down the street
Her eyes no longer have their childish innocence
She's a woman now
At least that's what the men say
After they raise themselves from atop her tiny body
She takes whatever they offer in return
A few dollars, a few rocks
It doesn't matter
Nothing matters to Lilly anymore
Lilly stops to watch a group of girls her age
on their way to school
laughing while they play their silly kid's games
Lilly knows she's not a child anymore
She can never go back to that
As she watches
Her head drops a little lower
Her heart feels a little heavier
Lilly keeps walking

Why Pray

Pray for the strength you need
Anytime you feel powerless or weak
When you feel sorrow or suffering
Pray for consolation and relief

When danger presents itself
Or Life's turmoils don't seem to cease
Pray for protection
Pray for peace

When you feel afraid
Or need someone to be near
Pray for comfort in times of loneliness
Pray for the courage to overcome your fears

When you're troubled by indecision
Or engulfed with weariness
Pray for Heavenly Guidance
Pray for time to rest

Pray that you'll find salvation
And do what God would have you do
Know that you are special
And I'll be praying for you

<u>Doshie Mae</u>

In my dreams
you laugh, you talk, you dance
just like you used to
you look so happy
that's why it breaks my heart to see you like this
confined to a wheelchair
barely able to stand
Silent
I know you want to speak to me
and I want to listen to everything I know you want to say but can't
I have so many questions now
There's so much I wanted to know--but was afraid to ask
I've grown up so much in these past few months since you were stricken
I've come to realize that so much of what you told me--and I
refused to believe--is true
I wish we could talk about these things...not as mother and
daughter..but as friends
I love you so much
the light in your eyes when you see me tells me that you love me
just as much
That should be enough--knowing that you love me
I guess I'm selfish because it's not
I want to hear you say 'Verily, Verily' in that funny way
I want you to dance to Bobbie Blue Bland or sing 'The Thrill is Gone'
I want to see you on the pews of the hymn choir in your red robe
That's the mama I miss

Nothing Between Us

I can see you clearly through this glass wall you've put between us
I see your sleepy eyes as you gaze dreamily in my direction
Is this a look of endearment or bewilderment?
I'm afraid to ask
Each time you speak, the bass in your voice makes this glass vibrate
even when you try to whisper
But you're careful not to speak too loudly
If this glass breaks it would leave you vulnerable
I'd be able to touch every part of you
You'd absorb all this love that I've been trying to give you for so long
You'd feel all my kisses, my caresses
You could no longer pretend not to hear what I'm saying
And you'd have to look me in the face
With nothing between us, could you then refuse my love?

Welcome

Welcome, my child
Welcome to the first day of your life
Tiny and perfect
You are all I dreamed you'd be

A few hours ago, I could not imagine feeling
as much Love as I feel right now
Yet, as I look into your twinkling eyes, just barely open
I can only weep

Beautiful baby of mine
I know that you will have troubles like we all do
But I will try to give you the courage to face them
And the knowledge to overcome them
All that I have, I will give to you, my child
In the hopes that you will share your gifts with those that you Love
If you are as happy in your lifetime as I am right now
I know that you will be blessed
Mommy Loves You

loving me

Something's wrong with my man

I don't understand the situation
I get no explanation

Calls from numbers I don't recognize
Out with the boys late at night

When your Lover's affections wane
It can drive a woman insane

It ain't easy to cope
It's hard to give up hope

But at some point you come to know
It's not worth it

The hurt starts to lift
Your focus starts to shift

It's time to think about you

IT'S A HOMICIDE

I can't believe...............!!!
Yes, I can
Why would you..................!!!
It doesn't matter
You did it AGAIN
You're apologizing AGAIN
You want me to pretend like nothing happened
AGAIN!!!
Well, it's not gonna happen like that AGAIN
This time, I'm gonna make sure you hurt
Just as much as I do
You're gonna understand
Once and for all
That you can't just go around treating people like trash
Using them, throwing them away
Lying to them
Treating them like they're stupid
Now, you're the stupid one
Do you feel stupid?
How stupid do you feel with a knife in your throat?
Does it hurt?
You make the world an ugly place
And you don't deserve to live

ASPHYXIA

At first, it feels like a vice gripping, pressing down
I never knew how much I took my breaths for granted
I try to steal a breath, but I can't
My eyes start to water
eventually they roll back, then flutter closed
As the rest of my body shuts down,
a peaceful feeling sweeps over me
I don't feel a thing

Who Do You Love?

Actually, the question is 'WHAT do you love?'
because I know you don't love me
As long as you have a 40 oz of something close by,
you're cool
As long as your friends think you're The Man and you have it
going on,
you're fine
As long as the ladies love you and want to give it to you, you're
feeling good
As long as there's a party somewhere and you're able to get your
groove on,
Life is Good
What I have to offer will never be enough for you
All I have is love and affection
security and faithfulness
a fruitful life
But it's not enough
That's not what you're looking for
What I'm offering is too Plain Jane---too Vanilla
I bore you
So I'm not going to hold you back
That's just not my way
You're free of me
I wish you nothing but happiness
in whatever bottle
at whatever party
or between whoever's legs
You find it

_C.S._

I need you, my friend
Real bad
Everything's broken
and I don't know how to fix it
I've never known much about men--
why they do the things they do
say the things they say
You helped bridge that gap
You told me things I needed to know
You helped me understand
Now I'm lost
and I don't have a clue where to turn
or what to do
You were the only man that's ever been totally honest with me
Good or Bad, you always told the truth
I could always trust you
I miss that so much
I miss YOU so much

Hard Loving

I cared so deeply
Loved so freely
That's all I ever wanted from you

I have asked for no thing
Not even a ring
Why do you do the things you do

You show no regard
Your manner is hard
Why must you be so cool
I give – you take
You proceed to make
Me look more and more like your fool

Come now, my love
This isn't fair
Do you not love me
Do you not care
That I need you badly
Love you so madly
Tell me why
No matter how hard I try
I can't get through
To any part of you

Untitled I

It was on a damp August night
-a long time ago-
When I first felt you peering through the shadows
I didn't know why you had come
but I was glad you were there
I would speak to you often
And even though I never caught a glimpse of your face
I knew you were listening
Each time a new Lover came into my life,
I would approach the edge of your shaded world
and share my excitement
But I would never attempt to enter
When my Love and I enjoyed eachother for the first time
I would whisper my secret to you in the dark
And when my Love no longer loved me
You knew that, too
You never criticized or shared any sentiment
You never made any effort to come to me
You just listened
And waited
As I addressed you one night with tears in my heart
I asked –"Why does Love always pass me by?"
You answered – "Love has found you but you do not recognize it.
It has not taken the form that you want. You've always been in
pursuit of what you love to look at rather than Love itself. Love
will only come where it's invited."
At that moment, I realized that you existed in the shadows only
because I had placed you there.
I held out my hand to you and invited you to walk with me in the
Light.

S & M

How can you say that you love me
when you know I don't feel the same
Why do you want to love me
when I've caused you so much pain

I constantly disrespect you
I hurt you just for spite
Deep down, you must know
That something isn't right

Still - you try to give me the World
moments after I've cursed you
When I say the sight of you makes me sick
you rush to try and nurse me

This relationship is perverse, at best
but this is the way we choose to live
I'll be the sadist and you – the masochist
taking whatever punishment I give

Untitled II

When you say
the things you say
to me
It Hurts.
How can you
not know?
You think that the
Lies you speak
about me
are funny.
But I can't find
the humor.
You criticize
everything
that I do.
I don't speak
the way you'd like.
I don't dress
to impress
You.
My friends
My music
My beliefs.......
You find them all
Bizarre
And you want to know
Why
I prefer being alone
Why
I don't want to be close
to you

Littlest Victims

The world is a cruel place for the little ones
We see them slumped over
Gripped by Hunger
And we look away with our bellies full
They suffer most
for all the injustices committed by those of us who
CHOOSE
to believe that no one will be affected
by our acts of hatred and greed
They are mercilessly battered
by cowards who'd dare not challenge an equal
They're indiscriminately mistreated
because someone else can not find happiness
We neglect them
Thinking that they'll somehow vanish
All of this is done to the Innocents
And We Wonder Why They're So Unforgiving

Before You Go

I've wanted to tell you how I feel for a very long time
But I was too embarrassed and ashamed to say it
Which is why I'm writing this letter
I realize that none of us are promised another day
I could not bear to let you leave me without knowing
I KNOW that it was hard raising all of your children
Especially Me
I'm sure you remember thinking that I resented you
for not being able to give me all the things
I thought I deserved
I said many things that hurt you
Not realizing that you were giving me more
than I deserved
A loving mother and a safe home
I know that I used to hurt you by acting like I was ashamed of you
But there's nothing shameful about having
A mother that would sacrifice her happiness
to make sure that her children always had a place to call Home
So before you go,
I just wanted to let you know
How very sorry I am
I love you more than you could ever know

<u>*Battered*</u>

Please forgive me, Lord
I've committed a terrible sin
I did not want to do it
but this nightmare had to end

I've killed a man tonight
in order to save myself
The last thing I recall
was lifting the gun from the shelf

I don't remember pulling the trigger
I don't remember the sound
I do remember his blank stare
as he lay motionless on the ground

I also remember the punches
the slaps, the shoves, the kicks
I'll never forget the sound of my screams
as I was begging him to quit

He didn't care if the kids were watching
He never cared what the neighbors would say
Whenever the police came to my "rescue"
He'd be back within a few days

It went on like this for months
and the months turned into years
I never knew what would set him off
so I lived in constant fear

Once, I summoned the courage to leave
I was ready for a new life to begin
But he found me, beat me and brought me back
And threatened to kill me if I tried it again

My days of suffering are over now
He has paid for all his cruel deeds
God, please grant him the Mercy
that he never had for me

Condemned

I step onto the oil stained pavement and I feel the hopelessness
start to smother me
I look at the should-be-condemned apartments that surround me
Sheets for curtains and ripped window screens
are the Norm
Before I know it, I'm walking
As I enter a sticky breezeway, the stench of piss and beer take my
breath away
I'm relieved to finally exit
And as I stop to catch my breath I hear voices behind me
I turn to see a group of young men sitting on the steps
They're all dressed in baggy jeans, Tims and hoodies
They drink 40's and talk about who got smoked last night
"Yeah, it was F'd up. You know, how it happened. But that shit
happen when you short the man. What you expect?"
They talk like I'm not even there
And I guess maybe I'm not
I go down the sidewalk to the building where I grew up
And it looks almost the same
except there's a step missing
I look up to the 2nd floor balcony and I see 2 girls
Yes, GIRLS
They're both pregnant
They both have crying babies on their hips
They walk past me on their way to the mailbox
I hear one of them say that she should get her check today
Then she can get her hair done and her nails done
After that, she'll get a ride to the mall so she can buy that leather
coat she saw last weekend
If she has some money left over, she'll buy her baby some of those
new sneakers
They only cost $50
I'm almost angry about her selfishness

Then I remember
She's a child so she thinks like one
If I hadn't lived it myself, I wouldn't believe that this type of
existence was possible
I guess I should be happy that I was able to escape
But it's hard to be happy when I know that some of these people
will live their whole lives here

Then and Now

Never had time to talk
Never a kind word to share
Never had time to listen
Never showed that you cared

Never wanted to love me
Never even tried
Never cared that it hurt
Never wiped the tears from my eyes

Never showed much interest
Never encouraged me to pursue my dreams
Never consoled me when I failed
Never applauded when I'd succeed

Never understood why
Never showed my shame
Never felt wanted
Never revealed the pain

Never created a memory
Never wanted to be bothered
Never was daddy's little girl
Never knew you, Father

Always see you on the street
Always look you in the eye
Always give a casual wave
Always pass you by

Always tell me I'm welcome in your home
Always have something to say
Always want to pull me close
Always puzzled when I look away

Always seem so genuine
Always wanting sympathy
Always denying that you're responsible
Always pointing the finger at me

Always, Never

I've always had a mother
She's never let me down
I've always had to make it without you
You chose never to come around

I'll always be scarred by your absence
You can never reverse what's been done
I'll always harbor resentment
There will never be a bond

I always closed my eyes and blew out my candles
But my wish never came true
I've outgrown my childish superstitions
I've outgrown any need for you

If this leaves you hurt, sad, or even lonely
You know how to soften the blow
Don't call, don't write, don't say I Love You
Pretend I'm still 10 years old

Message from Trey

I love you so much, Mother
More than I could ever show
More than I could ever say
More than you'll ever know

I know that you are missing me
As I am missing you
But my purpose there had been served
I now have greater things to do

I've put all our best memories inside this box
Put it where both you and Dad can see
Open it when you miss me most
You'll have happy thoughts of me

Although my physical body has left you
I never want you to fear
Because I've given you my Angels
And you know I'll always be near

I know that there's an emptiness
But there's no need for you to cry
I'm happy, I'm whole and I'm at peace
I'm waiting for you by His side

Just words

These are not words of wisdom
I don't aim to make you "feel" anything
There's no profound message in any of this
There's no rhyme, no story, no meaning
I've chosen to put these fifty seven words,
two quotation marks, four apostrophies,
five commas and one question mark
On this paper
Is this a poem?

To Dance With You Again

Staring at this candle's light, I'm reminded of the way we used to dance
Arms in air, feet barely touching the ground
Non-stop for hours on end
Too high from the heat to realize we're exhausted
I never thought I'd see the day you'd stop dancing
But the arms that used to twirl me are now limp
The feet that guided my steps are still
A stranger could mistake your gaze for intense adoration
I know it's a look of non-recognition
The person who knows me so well doesn't know me at all
I hate to see you like this
It would have been much easier for me to wait for the call
But I had to hold your hand
You become lucid enough to tell me what I've always known
But the finality with which you say these words confirms
The inevitable
I repeat those words to you and you're gone again
I never thought I'd see the day you'd stop dancing

Freedom

No matter what path you choose
You will be loved
You will be hated
So why worry about what people think?
If you want to sit back and just enjoy living
DO IT
If you want to start a revolution
MARCH ON
You are free to do whatever you like
You can cry as hard as you want or sing as loud as you want
IT'S OK
Dance like no one's looking, even if they are
Laugh like a maniac if that's what you're feeling
Wear what you want, Love who you want, Go where you want
DO WHAT YOU WANT
There's nothing wrong with being you
Accept yourself
Share your gifts
Find your peace
Happiness is what it's all about

Last Good-Bye

I would have kissed your lips a million times
And said "I Love You" many more
Held your hands, held you close
You wouldn't have walked out the door

I should have pressed my ear to your heart
And thanked God that you were alive
The most important day of my life and I didn't know it
It was our last good-bye

Writer's Block

Pen.
Paper.

Maybe Tomorrow.

In Utero

I want to go back
To my first space, my safest place
When I was immersed in the unconditional love that only Mothers
give

I wish for the time when
I was my mother's Best Friend
She was my Only Friend

I knew no fear, no pain
Sadness was still a stranger
Love was all I knew

Where is My Love?

Will he be waiting around the next corner?
Is he on the other side of this door that I'm about to open?
Maybe he's crossing the Atlantic as I write, counting the days until
he finds me
Does he know who I am?
Will it be love at first sight?
Where is My Love?

__Romantic__

Thunder in the distance
Lightning above
The river is singing my song
All my troubles are being swept away in this warm, humid breeze
All that's missing
Is you

Pretty Girls

Looks will get him- but will they keep him?
Your beauty makes him proud- but it does not make him Kind
Pretty girls get crushed
Pretty girls get lonely
Pretty girls do cry

Love Letter

I cried when I found them
Written so many years ago
I was a child
Yet every word rang true
They still do
Loved you then
Never stopped
I wanted to be yours forever - I am.
Missed you
Miss you more now that you are resting
I'm sending this love letter to you in Heaven
Hoping you haven't forgotten how much I Love You

Lovely

I've had a horrible day – a horrible week
Bills, PMS, everything's got me down
As I enter, I see it propped against the counter – misshapen
Not much care had been taken to paint it
In days past, it had nourished
It had grown
It was alive
I look past it and see a man almost as misshapen as his walking stick
His clothes aren't unusually fashioned, but they're soiled
Dry, peeling skin – all over his body
Swollen feet and ankles that have surely walked many more miles
than I in my short life
He, too, leans against the counter
Barely able to stand on his own
But he's smiling all the while
As he struggles to turn and reach his cane
He says "God Bless" to all
I conduct my business quickly and pass him on my way down the stairs
In my haste, I speed past—barely taking note of him
But he notices me
And halts to ask how I'm doing
I reply that I'm fine and out of courtesy – nothing more—
I ask how he's doing
"Lovely" he says
"Absolutely Lovely"

www.ingramcontent.com/pod-product-compliance
Lightning Source LLC
Chambersburg PA
CBHW021251280526
45784CB00005B/2330